# REDISCOVERING

# FAMILY WORSHIP

*Jerry Marcellino*

*Shepherd Press*
*Wapwallopen, Pennsylvania*

Shepherd Press
P.O. Box 24
Wapwallopen, PA 18660   USA
1-800-338-1445
www.shepherdpress.com

*11<sup>th</sup> printing, 2011*

# Introduction

*"Because the Christian is not his own, but bought with a price, he is to aim at glorifying God in every relation of life. No matter what station he occupies, or wherever he be, he is to serve as a witness for Christ. Next to the church of God, his own home should be the sphere of his most manifest devotedness unto Him. All its arrangements should bear the stamp of his heavenly calling. All its affairs should be so ordered that everyone entering it should feel 'God is here!'"*

— A.W. Pink

PROGRESS often makes people despise the past, as if it no longer offers anything of value. This is especially true in our own day, as we have progressed into the lonely age of iPods, the Internet, and cellular technology. Even among today's professing Christians there is a subtle rejection of historic Christianity, while remaining restlessly embedded in the shallow fads of modern Christianity. Christianity has taken on the attributes of a shallow culture without even knowing why. What will make the Christendom of this generation become once again a "salty" Christianity, as Matthew 5:13 calls it, a Christianity that is vital and acts as a preservative to a decaying society ? What can offer certain hope to a nation of families that are in utter disarray? Answer: A return to the old paths. It was the prophet Jeremiah who said,

*"...ask for the ancient paths, where the good way is, and walk in it; and you shall find rest for your souls"* (Jeremiah 6:16).

The Puritans in early America serve as a good example of a return to the old paths.

> *Let me now therefore, once more, before I finally cease to speak to this congregation, repeat, and earnestly press the counsel which I have often urged on the heads of families, while I was their pastor, to great painfulness in teaching, warning, and directing their children; bringing them up in the training and admonition of the Lord; beginning early, where there is yet opportunity, and maintaining constant dilligence in labours of this kind.*
>
> — Jonathan Edwards

# A LESSON FROM THE PAST

The Puritans of colonial New England were fond of comparing their venture in America to the genesis of Israel. They also believed that their flight from Europe was like the exodus out of Egypt; America herself was often called the Promised Land.[1] This "city-set-on-a-hill" community of believers in America was to be a light to the other nations of the world, just as God had intended Israel to be (Isaiah 49:6).

This pattern can be seen most clearly and importantly in the matter of family worship. Here, as in the Old Testament, the Puritan father was expected to be the religious leader of the home, enjoined by God Himself to lead his family daily in the worship of Jehovah. This practice was seen as the most primary function in preserving Christianity on early America's soil. And yet, as with Israel, less than a century had passed before this was the very realm in which backsliding was so prevalent. Listen to these observations from the past:

 ❑ In 1679 the Synod of New England gathered at Boston in response to a request by the General Court of the Massachusetts Colony to supply an answer to the following question: *What are the evils that have provoked the Lord to bring judgments upon New England?* These representative church leaders responded with fourteen reasons, the sixth of which reads:

*There are many families that do not pray to God constantly, morning and evening, and many more where the Scriptures are not daily read so that the Word of Christ might dwell richly in them. There are too many houses that are full of ignorance and profaneness and that are not duly examined and for this cause wrath may come upon others round about them as well as upon themselves (Joshua 22:20; Jeremiah 5:7; 10:25). Many householders who profess religion, do not cause all that are within their gates to become subject unto good order as they ought (Exodus 20:10).... Most of the evils that abound among us proceed from defects in family government.*[2]

◻  A century later, in 1766, the great American Baptist leader Isaac Backus (1724-1806) wrote for his generation:

*New England has formerly been a place famous for religion in general, and for family worship in particular. But of late, the neglect of this, as well as of other religious duties, has evidently been growing upon us; which has caused much grief to pious souls. But I have not heard that any discourse has been published upon this subject here these many years . . . as there have lately been numbers remarkably awakened in some parts of the land, who were trained up in the neglect of Family Prayer, and who are still at a loss about the Scriptural authority for the daily practice thereof.*[3]

◻  And in 1847 the venerable Presbyterian minister James W. Alexander commented about the obvious decline of this blessed duty:

*Our church cannot compare with that of the seventeenth century in this regard. Along with Sabbath-Observance, and catechizing of children, Family-Worship has lost ground. There are many heads of families, communicants in our churches, and (according to a scarcely credible report) some ruling elders and deacons, who maintain no stated daily service of God in their dwellings.*[4]

These sad reports from the seventeenth, eighteenth, and nineteenth centuries pale in comparison to the far worse observations that could be made in our own time. The decline has been steady with little to no recovery of the former zeal. And yet the Word of God tells us that such times will not always continue. Psalm 22:27 reminds us that someday *all the families of the nations shall worship before You.* With this hope in hand it is incumbent upon us to rekindle the fire that may well restore vital Christianity in our nation.

*It is highly honorable to family-worship, as a spiritual service, that it languishes and goes into decay in times when error and worldliness make inroads in the church.*
                                                    – James W. Alexander

*No man can approach the duty of leading his household in an act of devotion, without solemn reflection on the place which he occupies in regard to them. He is their head. He is such by Divine and unalterable constitution. These are duties and prerogatives which he cannot alienate.*

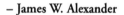

**– James W. Alexander**

# FOUR REASONS TO RESTORE FAMILY WORSHIP

Wh하t are the cogent reasons for restoring family worship in our churches? And, more importantly, why should you establish family worship in your own home? Below are four reasons:

## 1. We are Stewards of God's Gifts

The Psalmist says that children are literally gifts to us from the Lord (Psalm 127:3). This explains why God condemned the people in Jerusalem during Ezekiel's time for sacrificing their children to idols. In so doing they had destroyed His own precious possession. Listen:

> *Moreover, you took your sons and daughters, whom you had borne to Me, and you sacrificed them to idols to be devoured. Were your harlotries so small a matter? You slaughtered My children, and offered them up to idols by causing them to pass through the fire.*
>
> **Ezekiel 16:20–21**

Don't miss this important truth: Our children belong to God, and we are the divinely appointed stewards of these souls that will never die. We will be held responsible for what we do with the children He has placed under our care. This means we should use every means that God has given us to reach them with the gospel of our Lord Jesus Christ.

Such efforts will always be accompanied by a sense of spiritual responsibility to perpetuate the faith into the next generation (Psalm 78:1–8; Romans 14:7). Professor Neil Postman beautifully captured such a perspective when he said, *"Children are living messages that we send to a time we will not see."* [5]

> *Our hearts' desire toward our children ought to be as Paul's toward the Galatians, whom he called my children with whom I am again in labor until Christ is formed in you.*

It is God alone who grants us this stewardship for only a short while with the expectancy that we will be good stewards of these precious little gifts, so that we might raise them within a context of gospel influence to know Him, and then to make Him known, to the generations yet to be born (Psalm 22:30). Thus, God intends for us to propagate His kingdom, from generation to generation, primarily through godly families (Malachi 2:15).

Our hearts' desire toward our children ought to be like Paul's toward the Galatians, whom he called *"my children with whom I am again in labor until Christ is formed in you"* (Galatians 4:19). Paul is speaking here about those in the church — those who are regularly under the hearing of the Word. We should be like Paul, exercised to the point of experiencing labor pains until we see Christ formed in our children.

If Christ is our life, then in every breath that God gives to us, we will be seeking to bring Christ home to our children with our lives as well as with our words (Acts 13:36; Psalm 78:1–8; Malachi 2:15). The Scripture is quite clear: we must not live only for ourselves (Romans 14:7–9) but also for the generation to come (Psalm 102:18).

## 2. *Your Child is Placed in Your Home by Sovereign Design*

We must recognize God's good hand upon our children, by virtue of His having placed them into our believing homes. In fact, even if it is an unequally-yoked home in which only one of the parents is a believer, God's blessing is still upon that home. 1 Corinthians 7:12–14 explains:

> *If any brother has a wife who is an unbeliever, and she consents to live with him, let him not send her away. And a woman who has an unbelieving husband, and he consents to live with her, let her not send her husband away. For the unbelieving husband is sanctified through his wife, and the unbelieving wife is sanctified through her believing husband; for otherwise your children are unclean, but now they are holy.*

Your child cannot somehow "catch" salvation by osmosis or through the bloodlines. Rather, he is the recipient of a sanctifying influence from heaven by virtue of his being placed within the sphere of gospel influence. Therefore, because of God's sovereign grace and His providential design, some children are placed in a home where the gospel is lived and taught, this should give every believing parent good reason to hope that God intends to save them (John 5:34; 2 Peter 3:15).

Paul continues in 1 Corinthians 7:16: *"For how do you know, O wife, whether you will save your husband? Or how do you know, O husband, whether you will save your wife?"* In other words, if your unbelieving spouse consents to live with you, don't send him or her away — be glad for the opportunity to still influence them. And if a believing spouse can influence an unbelieving spouse, then it is certain that a single believing parent can also influence his or her children.

Timothy is a good case in point. Acts 16:1 tells us that he was raised in an unequally-yoked home, having an unbelieving Greek father, and yet his believing mother and grandmother successfully taught him the Scriptures that were able to give him the *"wisdom that leads to salvation through faith which is in Christ Jesus"* (2 Timothy 3:15). Timothy became a powerful minister of the gospel, greatly used by God despite having an unbelieving father.

Now we must not just simply acknowledge God's sovereign orchestration in our homes; we must also use every God-ordained means to reach our little ones, by seeking in a responsible way to initiate and consistently cultivate the daily worship of God with our families.

Indeed, God commands this ideal. He says in Ecclesiastes 12:1, *"Remember also your Creator in the days of your youth."* How else is a child going to know his Creator in his youth apart from his parent's daily bringing Christ near to him? God desires for parents to use every available means to reach their children while they are young, when they are tender and most naturally influenced by their parents, especially through their natural affections toward them.

## 3. Family Worship Prepares Us for Public Worship

Family worship, however, does not stand on its own. We must understand that it is one essential part of a threefold approach to worshiping God, comprised of private, family, and public worship. Only our private worship of God, which is the beginning point and foundation for all that we do as Christians, will sufficiently prepare us to influence the family He has so graciously given to us.

Our own lives must be godly, consistent, and loving examples to our children, full of joy and praise of God. As such examples we will seek to bring God and His Word into our homes with praise. We will strive at all times to press home thoughts about God, to speak of the glory of God, and to give praise to God. And if these things are done consistently in our home, there is a much greater likelihood that such a family will come to God's house on the Lord's Day ready to offer fervent worship to Him, in spirit and in truth (John 4:19–24).

*The lifelessness experienced in so many churches in our day can be traced directly to the multitudes of families in those churches which contain Sunday-morning Christians only.*

Since the family has already been worshiping God the previous six days in both private and family worship, public worship will be a natural outflow. Children in a home like this will know that worship is not just something you turn on and off. Worship will be understood by them as being in all of life (Deuteronomy 6:6-9). They will experience the beginning and/or the culmination of each day's spiritual activities within their home in a "family worship service," including praise, prayer, and the Word.

They will learn early in such a worshipful and fruitful home that the

Lord's Day is a blessed day, the crescendo of all that they have been doing throughout their week — worshiping God in all of life!

The lifelessness experienced in so many churches in our day can be traced directly to the multitudes of families in those churches that contain only Sunday-morning Christians . It is plain to see the reason for such deadness when these individuals are not consistently worshiping God in private. Statistics reveal that only eleven percent of all professing Christians in America read their Bible or some portion of it once a day. If so few professing Christians are spending time alone with God, it should not be surprising that family worship as a practice among professing Christian families is practically nonexistent.

If fathers are experiencing the presence of God daily, and growing in their love for Christ, it will be evidenced by their leadership at home. Surely then, public worship on the Lord's Day will be transformed by such vitality.

## 4. The Spiritual Decline of Our Nation

Hear Joshua's challenge to the nation of Israel:

> *Now therefore, fear the Lord and serve Him in sincerity and truth, and put away the gods which your fathers served beyond the River and in Egypt, and serve the Lord. And if it is disagreeable in your sight to serve the Lord, choose for yourselves today whom you will serve: whether the gods which your fathers served which were beyond the River, or the gods of the Amorites in whose land you are living; but as for me and my house, we will serve the Lord.*
>
> Joshua 24:14–15

Many years ago, in the nation of Greenland, there was an interesting custom that was practiced every time a stranger would knock on someone's door. The inhabitant would naturally ask,

"*Who is there?*" And then the stranger would respond, "*Is God in your house?*" If the answer was *yes*, he would enter that house.[6]

An individual was once heard to say, "*As the home goes, so goes the church, and so goes the nation.*"

If someone were to come to your house today and ask you "Is God in your house?", what would you say? Is He the life and breath of your family? Is He precious, or at least becoming precious, to everyone in your home? Is the name of Jesus Christ exalted there?

Why is our nation so godless? Why are most churches in our day so spiritually apathetic? Why are the homes of many professing believers in our day in spiritual disunity, mere shells of formality ? The Bible tells us that one of the major reasons for this grievous decline is that our churches, in general, are void of men who have resolved, like Joshua, to lead their families daily in the worship of the living God.

Paul told the men in the church of Corinth to *act like men* (1 Corinthians 16:13). In our day true manhood has been given a carnally twisted redefinition. But the Bible describes the true head of the home as one who leads his family in the daily worship of the living God (Ephesians 6:4). If you are not sure how to do that, is it at least your desire to learn how? Is a contemplation of the eternal welfare of the souls beneath your roof enough to move you to duty?

Scripture teaches that the church is the key determiner as to whether men will act like true men. When the church begins to be the church, led by men of spirit given backbone who will be reproducers of like men, then we can expect that there will ultimately be a leavening effect on the whole of Christendom!

Why is God presently judging our nation? Individual families within the churches of our nation have followed the idolatrous ways of the world and have forsaken the daily worship of the living God within their homes! Therefore, the church has become like the world. Jeremiah 10:25 says:

> *Pour out Thy wrath on the nations that do not know Thee, and on the families that do not call Thy name ...*

Why?

> *...For they have devoured Jacob; they have devoured him and consumed him, and have laid waste his habitation.*

God says that families cumulatively make up nations. And when nations are under judgment, it can be fairly deduced that their widespread failure to worship the living God, as families, is the cause! Therefore, wrath is sent upon the homes of a nation. In fact, such spiritual neglect of the souls in families is tantamount to devouring, consuming, and laying waste a nation!

But such wrath is also the result of the sin of selfishness. Romans 14:7–9 says,

> *For not one of us lives for himself, and not one dies for himself; for if we live, we live for the Lord, or if we die, we die for the Lord; therefore whether we live or die, we are the Lord's. For to this end Christ died and lived again, that He might be Lord both of the dead and of the living.*

Why did Jesus die? He died that He might produce a people who would be zealous for Him—a people who would not just live for themselves but as servants to others, especially as they see their role in the unfolding of God's redemptive plan. As you raise your children to know God, don't forget that they will be parents one day. They will also raise their children—your grandchildren—who will in turn raise your great-grandchildren! God is not only judging us in our day—He will judge them in theirs.

# GETTING STARTED

I f family worship is to be successfully established, both the recognition of its priority and a zeal for its continuity should be the bedrock conviction of both father and mother. In other words, ideally, worshiping God together as a family must flow from individual hearts who truly desire to see Jesus lifted up in their home.

## *How Do You Establish Family Worship in the Home?*

The establishment of family worship in the home begins with a conviction and then moves to action.

Family worship must be seen as an integral part of each family's daily spiritual responsibilities. But remember, consistency and flexibility are keys to its endurance. In order to avoid frustration and ultimately failure, it is vital that the father, as head of the home, discern how family worship can best be applied in his own family.

## *Who Is to Participate?*

The participants in family worship are all those who constitute a particular family. In other words, it may mean a young husband and wife without children, or an older couple whose children have already left home. It includes both believing and unbelieving spouses (as much as possible), and certainly family worship can be led by a single parent (Acts 16:1).

It is to include all of the children who are at home, regardless of their ages. All family members can derive great spiritual benefit, even the very young. By just listening and watching, they are learning the priority of worship in their lives. Remember that the practice of family worship could blossom into the very instrument that brings them to Christ (2 Timothy 3:15). Family worship will present them with a forum for healthy and thoughtful reflection on, interaction over, digestion of, and, hopefully, application of the Scriptual truths necessary for the eternal welfare of their souls.

## *Where is Family Worship to Take Place?*

Deuteronomy 6:7 gives us much freedom in this area:

> *And you shall teach them* [God's commands] *diligently to your sons and shall talk of them when you sit in your house and when you walk by the way and when you lie down and when you rise up.*

Once again, a family's particular living situation must be considered. The home environment is best for its consistency, flexibility, resiliency and immediate availability. However, our family has worshiped together at a favorite park, a beautiful cemetery nearby, in our living room, family room, various bedrooms, and even in our own backyard. Each of those places offers us refreshing alternatives to our normal daily setting, which is at the kitchen table after clearing the breakfast or dinner dishes. We also enjoy worshiping in our family library where we often read individually and together.

## *When Does Family Worship Take Place?*

In a general sense, family worship should be going on all the time in a spiritually healthy home (Read Deuteronomy 6:6-9). But

14

it is crucial to have a specific regular time, which fits each particular family's daily schedule. For some families mornings are impossible; after dinner is their choice. For others, after breakfast is the best time. Morning is probably the time of day with the least distractions for most families (Most phone calls and drop-in visitors tend to occur at evening time). But if you are not flexible and resilient, with all that life might throw your way in a typical day, you will be frustrated and give up after just getting out of the starting blocks! Remember here again, consistency, flexibility, resiliency and immediate availability are the important factors.

# The Three Key Elements of Family Worship

The elements primarily available to the father (or other head of household) as he leads family worship are the same as those found in weekly public worship. At a minimum these three are most essential and should be included: song, Scripture, and supplication.

## 1. *Worshiping in Song*

The Lord is to be worshiped in song. Psalm 69:30 says, *I will praise the name of God with song, and shall magnify Him with thanksgiving.*

In family worship we should lead our family in singing to the Lord because He is pleased when we praise Him! For those who feel they cannot sing or are not musically inclined, there are resources available to assist you in making music a part of your daily worship time (See information regarding helpful resources at the end of this booklet).

Sing often the songs that your children are learning in Sunday School and on other occasions with their peers. The Psalms, hymns, and spiritual songs which are often sung in the public worship services of your church should also be sung. In fact, if more families sang the praises of God together in their homes, just think how much our congregational singing on the Lord's Day might improve!

Another good idea is to conclude each family worship time together with singing the doxology or some other praise-filled chorus. Martin Luther demonstrated how important he felt music was in the worship of God, whether it was offered at home or among the gathered assembly, when he said, *...next to the Word of God, music deserves the highest praise...* [7]

## 2. *Worshiping with Scripture*

Scriptural instruction is central. The Word of God is to be at the center in family worship. Our goal should be to help the members of our family develop a love for God's Word, with the hope that they will begin to feed upon every word of it (Matthew 4:4).

Remember that God's Word is to be taught reverently and creatively, as well as with much animation. Strive never to bore your children with your delivery of God's Word to them. Be thoughtful in how you illustrate or paint pictures of the main points. Ask them plenty of easy questions (laced with a few difficult ones to make them think hard!). You will be surprised to find that children are very able to stay with you as you teach. Hold the standard high, and God will bring them to it. Labor to make each teaching time a lesson for them to remember.

There are a variety of ways God's Word can be conveyed to your family:

1. By direct reading from the Bible according to a plan.
2. By reading from a sound Bible story book.
3. Through the use of a catechism, a very successful method of teaching biblical truths by simple questions and answers.
4. Through Scripture memory and review.

5. By reading from a good devotional commentary.
6. By reading through solid Christian classics like *The Pilgrim's Progress* (Make sure your Bibles are in front of you, to explore the scriptural truths that will jump from every page).
7. By reading from various types of Christian literature: biographies, historical fiction, or theologically based novels.

Again, some fathers may feel inadequate in this area, but where God has given responsibility, he also provides the ability to accomplish it. For the father who is truly commited, where there is a will, there is a way.

### 3. *Worshiping by Supplication*

Supplications are to be offered in Jesus' name. We are to teach our children to pray not only by the example of the words we use in our prayers, but also by supplying them with information to be prayed about. Pray often for the needs of your family and extended family (especially the unsaved), for the needs of families

> *God has so designed that children, in their formative years, naturally look to their fathers in order to emulate them, since they are the ones who protect and provide for them.*

in your local congregation, the spiritual needs of our nation, and for the dire needs of a lost world (both locally and internationally). The list could go on . . . ad infinitum! Remember, we are teaching our children to take little steps toward God as we

17

illustrate our own dependence upon Him in our prayers.

## How Long Should it Be?

The length of the worship time depends upon a number of factors, such as the number of children, their ages, and the attention span of the group. Some parents with small children may feel that ten minutes is just perfect for their family in the early stages of implementing family worship at home. For others, though they desire to spend more time, ten minutes is all they can fit in their schedule. Some families are able to have a profitable thirty minutes.

> *Let family worship be short, savory, simple, plain, tender, heavenly.*
>
> – Richard Cecil

A good goal to shoot for is *fifteen to twenty* minutes. Whatever your time limits are, be sure it is a time where you focus, as a family on the Son of the living God.

# Making Family Worship Effective

The practice of daily family worship offers many advantages to the parent who is trying to reach his children with the gospel. For one thing, God has designed that children, in their formative years, naturally tend to look to their fathers in order to emulate them, since they are the ones who protect and provide for them.

Before the heavy onslaughts of the world come upon them, children are already naturally bent toward hearing their parents, especially their fathers. In their formative years they are not listening more carefully to the President than to their parents. They are not yet listening to and embracing accepted societal norms. Rather they are in essence saying to their parents, "Mold me—impart to me what's most precious to your hearts."

But so often a child sees behind all of the religious garb of his parents and finds what is really precious to them! He sees patterns of heart which lure them toward a pursuit of wealth, leisure, entertainment, shopping, or religious busyness. A child can easily see when these things are more exciting to his parents than devotion to Jesus Christ! When this proves to be the case, a child will embrace those same affections—to the detriment of his own soul!

However, when children see that their parents are people who pant after God—parents who are constantly poring over the Scriptures and going to God in prayer about everything—parents who have a proper balance between the enjoyment of life and seeking to conform everything to bring glory to God—their children can be expected to adopt that same balance. Whatever or whoever is precious to you, will be precious to your children.

Notice this principle that can be drawn from 1 Timothy 4:16 and applied to every father:

> *Pay close attention to yourself and to your teaching;*
> *Persevere in these things; for as you do this you will insure*
> *salvation both for yourself and for those who hear you.*

Based on God's Word, fathers are responsible to be the shepherds, or pastors, of their own homes. Therefore this text applies, in principle at least, to fathers as well as to the elders of the local church.

Fathers then should pay close attention to their private worship as well as to their teaching in family worship. It may well be that the real reason fathers are not leading their homes in the daily worship of the living God is because they are not having their own heart dealings with God, alone and on a daily basis. They are not being priests because they are not studying God's Word for the health of their own souls, let alone interceding for their families on a regular basis. The great French reformer J.H. Merle d'Aubigne gave this challenge:

> *My brethren, is there an altar in your hearts erected to the only living and true God? Are you the temple of God and does God's Spirit dwell within you? So long as there is no altar erected to God in your souls, there can be none in your houses.*[8]

For this reason it is not surprising that so many homes are in spiritual disarray.

John Geree wrote this about a typical Puritan father in 1646:

> *His family he endeavored to make a church, both in regard of persons and exercises, admitting none into it but such as feared God; and laboring that those that were born in it, might be born again to God.*

To the Puritans family life was enormously important:

> *... a family is the seminary of church and state and if children be not well principled there, all miscarrieth. . . keep up the government of God in your families: holy families must be the chief preservers of the interest of religion in the world.*[9]

Have you considered that our homes are in essence little seminaries? The theological tutor of this seminary is the father (Proverbs 22:6; Ephesians 6:4). Just how does he accomplish this?

> *Only a disciple can make a disciple.*
>
> —A.W. Tozer

Primarily, by leading his family in the daily worship of the living God.

Now is the time for believing parents to implement daily family worship, even though it is a foreign concept to most of modern-day evangelicalism. Parents, and in particular fathers, must see that they are primarily responsible for the spiritual training of their children—not the Sunday school teacher, youth worker, or pastoral staff. Thus, take up, without delay, your God-given responsibility to lead your little ones to God!

## *Family Worship Revived*

Some of us come from families that cursed rather than worshiped the Savior. Others might have grown up in a pseudo-Christian home where Christ was only on our lips for a few hours on Sunday. Still others have come from homes that were faithful to the light given them, but still knew nothing of family worship. Don't be discouraged; rather, by the grace of God be determined to be a catalyst for turning this generation around (Acts 13:36). May God be pleased to raise up a generation of Josiahs following this generation of Manassehs (2 Chronicles 34–35; 2 Kings 22:1–23:28). Families that worship God can change churches—yes, even nations (Psalm 22:27)!

May our continual prayer to God be that He would fill this land once again with churches like the Puritan church in Dorchester, Massachusetts, whose members made the following resolution in 1677:

> *We covenant, as a church in Dorchester, Massachusetts, to reform our families, engaging ourselves to a conscientious care to set up and maintain the worship of God in our homes. And to walk in our homes with perfect hearts. We resolve, in*

**21**

> *a faithful discharge of all domestic duties in seeking to*
> *educate, instruct and charge our little ones and our whole*
> *households to seek to keep the ways of the Lord.*[10]

May the living and true God give us that same resolve, and then, in mercy, grant us the spiritual awakening we so desperately need.

> *Lord, I have heard the report about Thee and I fear.*
> *O Lord, revive Thy work in the midst of the years,*
> *In the midst of the years make it known;*
> *In wrath remember mercy.*

**Habakkuk 3:2**

*If the parent be not visibly in earnest, it*
*cannot be expected that the child will be so.*
— John Angell James

# *End Notes*

1. Cotton Mather, *The Great Works of Christ in America*, 2 vols. (Carlisle, PA: Banner of Truth Trust, 1979 [1702]), 1:48.

2. Richard Owen Roberts, *Sanctify the Congregation* (Wheaton: International Awakening Press, 1994), p. 24.

3. Alvah Hovey, *The Life and Times of the Reverend Isaac Backus* (Harrisonburg, VA: Gano Books, 1991 [1858]), p. 149.

4. J.W. Alexander, *Thoughts on Family Worship* (Morgan, PA: Soli Deo Gloria Publications, 1990, pp. 1-2.

5. Neil Postman, *The Disappearance of Childhood* (New York, NY: Vintage Books, 1994 [1982]), p.xi.

6. Thomas Watson and Samuel Lee, *The Bible and the Closet* (Harrisonburg, VA: Sprinkle Publications, 1992 [1842]), p. 7.

7. Pelikan, Jarslov and Lehman, H.T. eds., *Luther's Works*, 55 Vols. (St. Louis, MO: Concordia Publishing House; Philadelphia, PA: Fortress Press, 1955-1986), 53:323.

8. J.H. Merle d'Aubigne, *Family Worship* (Dallas: Presbyterian Heritage Publications, 1989 [1827]), p. 25.

9. J.I. Packer, *Quest for Godliness* (Wheaton: Crossway Books, 1990), p. 270.

10. Leland Ryken, *Worldly Saints* (Grand Rapids: Zondervan, 1986), p. 80.

*Soli Deo Gloria!*

*Notes:*

25